Introduction

Finger knitting is fast, easy, and so much fun! The basic technique is incredibly simple, but you can use it to produce tons of fabulous looks. With just a skein of yarn, you can create pieces suitable for a casual day of shopping, a festive night out, or a sophisticated day at the office.

You may think finger knitting is just for scarves, but it can be used for so much more! Add some beads and you can create a totally unique necklace or belt. Use the finger chaining technique to create a headband. Or add a piece of finger knitting to a wreath or throw pillow for a soft, cozy accent piece. This book is full of ideas to take your finger knitting to the next level.

Finger knitting is also the perfect way to make custom pieces that match your personal taste and style. You can create tons of different looks just by changing the yarn you use, the color scheme you select, or the embellishments you add. Fat, chunky yarns will produce cozy scarves with great bulk to keep out the winter chill, while thin, delicate yarns are perfect for lacy fashion necklaces you can wear year round. Choose yarns in bright colors for a fresh and fun look, or select neutrals for a more sophisticated style. Embellishments are another way to change up the look. Whether it's tassels, pom-poms, beads, or buttons, you're sure to find something that you love.

So whether you need an accessory to go with your favorite outfit or a new home décor piece for your apartment, finger knitting will help you make it!

Happy knitting!

About Metric

Throughout this book, you'll notice that every measurement is accompanied by a metric equivalent. Inches and feet are rounded off to the nearest half or whole centimeter unless precision is necessary (note that some larger measurements are rounded off to the nearest meter). Please be aware that while this book will show 1 yard = 100 centimeters, the actual conversion is 1 yard = 90 centimeters, a difference of about 3 15/16" (10cm). Using these conversions, you will always have a little bit of extra yarn if measuring using the metric system.

Contents

This variation on the pom-pom scarf is super easy. Finger knit a piece long enough to wrap around your neck several times. Bind off and sew the finger knitting together in a loop. Weave in the ends. Loop the scarf to form several wraps; then join the wraps using a leather bracelet blank held closed with jump rings. Glue could also be used.

Finger knit a piece long enough to wrap around your neck several times. Bind off and weave in the ends. Make two tassels following the instructions on page 18. Tie or sew a tassel to each end of the scarf.

Opposite Page:
Pom-Pom Scarf

Beaded Mod Necklace

Super Chunky Bracelets (see page 20). To make the necklace, use two strands of super bulky weight yarn held together to finger knit on four stitches for 10" (25cm) or until the necklace reaches the desired length. Bind off and weave in the ends. Sew two lengths of thin ribbon to each end of the finger knitting for ties. Cover the ends of the ties by wrapping each end of the necklace with a piece of wide ribbon, stitching it in place.

Getting Started

A single strand of yarn will allow you to finger knit pieces that you can transform into tons of different projects! In this section, you'll find everything you need to get started with finger knitting, plus some additional techniques to take your projects to the next level!

Casting On

1| Start the slip knot. Measure in several inches from the end of the yarn and form a slip knot. Start by forming a loop with the yarn. Then twist it so the strands cross at the bottom.

2| Complete the slip knot. Reach through the loop, grab the top strand, and pull it through, forming a new loop. Tighten the knot by gently tugging on the loose ends.

3| Anchor the slip knot. Put the slip knot on your left thumb and tighten it slightly so it is snug against your thumb but not too tight. The slip knot simply anchors the yarn on your hand to make knitting easier.

4| Weave one row. Bring the yarn over your left index finger, under your middle finger, over your ring finger, and under and around your pinky. Then, bring the yarn under your ring finger, over your middle finger, and under and around your index finger.

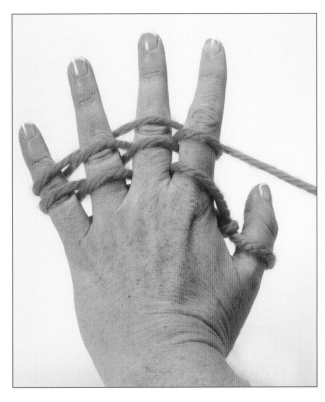

5| Weave one more row. Repeat the weaving pattern to create one more row. When finished, the yarn should be back at your thumb where it started, and you should see two loops on each finger.

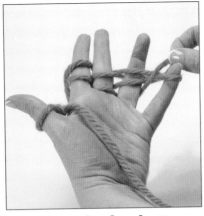

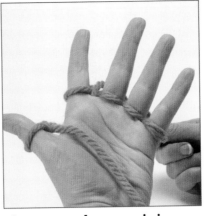

1| Remove the first bottom loop. After casting on, turn your hand so you are looking at your palm. You will see two loops on each finger. Starting with your pinky, lift the bottom loop over the top loop and off your finger. This will leave just one loop on your finger.

2| Remove the remaining bottom loops. Repeat with the loops on your remaining fingers, lifting the bottom loop over the top loop and off your finger for each one. This completes the first row. You can now remove the slip knot loop from your thumb as the yarn is anchored on your fingers.

3| Weave the yarn. Continue working with your palm facing you. Weave the yarn over and under your fingers for one row as described for casting on. When finished, you should see two loops on each finger.

4| Remove the bottom loops. Lift the bottom loop on each finger over the top loop and off your finger. When finished, you will have one loop on each finger. This completes the second row.

5| Repeat. Continue weaving the yarn over and under your fingers and then lifting the bottom loop off each finger to add rows. As you work, your project will grow off the back of your hand. Occasionally tug on the tail of yarn at the back of your hand to snug up the project as you work.

Tip

Make sure the yarn loops are not too tight around your fingers as you work. Keep them loose so you can easily lift them off to form each row and remove them from your fingers when you are finished.

Basic Stitch: Variation 2

1| Make the first row. Repeat steps 1–2 of Basic Stitch: Variation 1 to complete the first row. When finished, you will see one loop on each finger.

2| Wrap the yarn. Continue working with your palm facing you. Wrap the yarn once around all four fingers. You should see two rows.

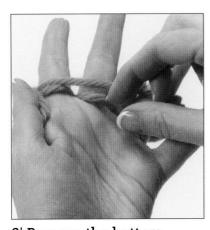

3| Remove the bottom loops. Lift the bottom loop on each finger over the top yarn wrap and off your finger. When finished, you will have one loop on each finger. This completes the second row.

4| Repeat. Continue wrapping the yarn around your fingers and then lifting the bottom loop off each finger to add rows. As you work, your project will grow off the back of your hand. Occasionally tug on the tail of yarn at the back of your hand to snug up the project as you work.

Stitch Variations

You will see a subtle difference between pieces created using the two stitch variations. Variation 1 (right) takes a little more effort to knit, but the final result is a bit more polished. Variation 2 (left) can be knit very quickly, but the stitches might not appear as even. Use Variation 1 for projects where the finished stitches will be highly visible. If you just want to whip up a quick piece of finger knitting to transform into something else, use Variation 2. Also, if you're finger knitting with kids, Variation 2 is quick and easy for them to learn.

Binding Off

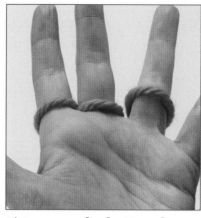

1| Move the first loop. Once your project reaches the desired length, you are ready to bind off. Complete a row so you have one loop on each finger. Then, lift the loop off of your pinky and put it on your ring finger so you have two loops on your ring finger.

2| Remove the bottom loop. Lift the bottom loop on your ring finger over the top loop and off your finger. This will leave just one loop on your ring finger.

3| Repeat and finish. Continue moving each loop over from one finger to the next and then removing the bottom loop until you are left with two loops on your index finger. Remove the bottom loop as before, and then lift the remaining loop off of your index finger, holding it in place. Trim the working end of the yarn and pull it through the loop. Tug on the yarn to tighten the knot.

Switching Colors

Switching colors in finger knitting is super easy! Work a section of finger knitting in your first color. When you're ready to switch colors, complete a row and trim the working yarn of the color you're using, leaving an 8" (20cm) tail. Use yarn in your second color to weave or wrap rows on your fingers following Variation 1 or 2 of the Basic Stitch. Be sure to leave an 8" (20cm) tail when you add your second color. Work a section of finger knitting using the new color you just added. Switch colors again as desired using this technique. After binding off, tie the tails at any place you switched colors together using an overhand knot. Tie the knot as close to the edge of your project as possible, and then weave in the tails as shown on page 13.

Weaving in Ends

When you finish a project, you will have some loose ends of yarn attached to it from your cast-on and bind-off tails, or perhaps from switching colors. These ends can be woven into the stitches of your project to hide them and to give your piece a clean, finished look.

1| Thread a strand. Thread one of the loose ends you need to weave in onto a tapestry needle. If there is a knot at the base of the end you are weaving in, use the needle to bring the loose end through the knot, going from the outer edge of the piece toward the inside.

2| Split the plies. Follow the end you need to weave in back into the work and find a stitch near the edge that has a strand of the same color. Use the tip of the needle to split the plies of the stitch strand and bring the loose end through them. (Plies are just the individual strands that are twisted together to form the yarn.)

3| Finish and trim. Weave the loose end through the plies of the stitch strand for several inches. Then, trim the loose end close to the stitch strand. Repeat steps 1–3 with the remaining loose ends, weaving each one into a different stitch strand. Do not weave multiple ends into the same stitch strand.

4| Hide any knots. Hide any knots by tucking them into the center of the piece. When you are finished, you will have a seamless piece with no loose ends dangling from it!

Sewing Edges Together

You can transform a piece of finger knitting into a flat disk by spiraling it around itself several times and sewing the edges together. This is perfect for making home décor pieces like rugs or coasters.

1| Stitch the first fold. Thread a tapestry needle onto the bind-off tail. Then fold the first inch or so (3cm) of the tail end of the finger knitting back on itself. Find two loops opposite one another where the edges of the fold touch and stitch through them with the needle, trying not to split the plies.

2| Repeat. Repeat, continuing to fold the piece around itself and stitch the edges together where they touch. As you work, don't pull the stitches too tight, or the piece might pucker. Stop every few inches to lay the piece down and make sure it is flat and not forming a cupped shape.

Bracelet Closure

Make a quick and easy closure by tying the final stitch of the bind-off into a loop with an overhand knot. Leave a 7" (18cm) cast-on tail and tie an overhand knot at the very end of it to prevent fraying. Use the tail and loop to tie the bracelet onto your wrist.

Finger Chaining

Once you have completed a long piece of finger knitting, you can finger chain it to form an even more decorative piece that can be used as a necklace, belt, headband, or anything else you want! Start with a piece of finger knitting at least 72" (185cm) long or longer.

1| Make a slip knot. Follow steps 1–2 from Casting On (page 9) to form a slip knot with your completed finger knitting piece. Adjust the ends so you have a short tail and a long working end.

2| Grab the working end. Reach through the loop of the slip knot and grab the working yarn.

3| Pull up a new loop. Pull a portion of the working yarn through the slip knot loop, forming a new loop.

4| Repeat. Reach through the new loop, grab the working yarn, and pull a portion through to form a new loop. Repeat until the chain reaches the desired length.

5| Finish. To finish the chain, reach through the current loop, grab the working yarn, and pull all of it through the loop. Tug on the yarn to tighten the knot.

Beaded Fringe

You can easily add beaded fringe to any project, but it looks especially great on a belt. If you're planning to add fringe, make sure you leave a very long tail (at least 12" [30cm] long) at the beginning and end of your project.

1| Start adding the fringe.
The tails at each end of your project serve as fringe. Add some more fringe pieces by cutting additional strands of yarn twice as long as the desired length of the fringe, plus 2" (5cm). Take one strand and fold it in half to form a loop at the center.

2| Finish adding the fringe.
Feed the loop through one of the stitches at the end of your project. Bring the ends of the strand through the loop and tug on them gently to tighten the knot. Repeat with the remaining strands until you have the desired amount of fringe on each end of your project.

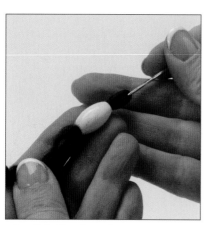

3| Add the beads. Thread a tapestry needle onto one of the fringe strands and use it to feed the strand through your chosen beads. You can add beads randomly or in a specific pattern. Remove the needle and tie two overhand knots after the last bead to secure the beads in place.

4| Finish. Repeat to bead all of the fringe strands at one end of your project. Once all the strands have been beaded, trim the ends even. Bead the fringe strands at the other end of your project if desired.

Flower

Transform a piece of finger knitting into an adorable yarn flower that you can use as an embellishment on any project. Start with a 28" (70cm)-long piece of finger knitting with an extra long bind-off tail.

1| Form the loops. Thread a tapestry needle with the bind-off tail from your finger knitting piece. Then, form the petals with the finger knitting piece by making five overlapping loops approximately 1½" (5cm) tall around a central point.

2| Stitch the loops. Use the bind-off tail and tapestry needle to stitch the loops together where they overlap at the center point of the flower.

3| Add a button. Add a button at the center of the flower. Bring the needle through the hole in the button (shank button shown), and then stitch through the center of the flower. Repeat several times until the button is secure.

4| Finish. Finish by making three stitches at the back of the flower. Remove the tapestry needle, but do not trim the tail. Use the tail to sew or tie your flower to a project.

Tassel

1| Prepare the cardboard. Cut a piece of cardboard with a height equal to the desired height of the top of the finished tassel; the width does not matter. Cut a 12"–15" (30–40cm) length of yarn. Place the yarn widthwise in the center of the cardboard.

2| Prepare the strands. Cut eight strands of yarn twice as long as the desired length of the finished tassel. Fold them in half over the cardboard and the 12"–15" (30–40cm) length of yarn as shown.

3| Knot the strands together. Cut a 20" (50cm)-long piece of yarn and place it behind the tassel strands at the bottom edge of the cardboard. Tie an overhand knot around the strands as close to the cardboard as possible. Then tie a second overhand knot on top of the first.

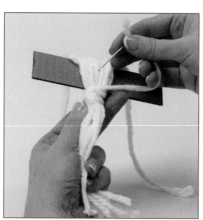

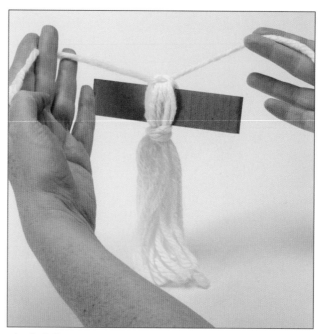

4| Secure the ends. Take one end from the overhand knot and wrap it around the overhand knot one to two times. Thread the cut end through a tapestry needle and use the needle to bring the yarn through the wrap around the overhand knot. Remove the needle. Repeat with the other end.

5| Finish. Tie the 12"–15" (30–40cm) strand in a loose overhand knot. Use this stand to attach the tassel to your project. Remove the cardboard, and trim the ends of the hanging strands even.

Pom-Pom

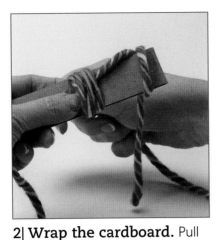

1| Prepare the cardboard. Cut a piece of cardboard with a width equal to half the desired diameter of the finished pom-pom; the height does not matter. Cut a 12"–15" (30–40cm) length of yarn to tie your pom-pom. Place the yarn in the center of the cardboard as shown.

2| Wrap the cardboard. Pull a strand of yarn from a skein and wrap it around the cardboard as shown as many times as desired. The more wraps you make, the fuller your pom-pom will be. Let the ends of the 12"–15" (30–40cm) strand of yarn hang loose as you wrap.

3| Tie the pom-pom. Once you've wrapped the cardboard as many times as desired, take the ends of the 12"–15" (30–40cm) strand and use them to tie a square knot over the wraps. Make the knot as tight as possible. Cut the end of the wrapping strand from the skein.

4| Cut the wraps. Remove the cardboard, keeping the wraps in place around your fingers. Cut the wraps apart using scissors. Sharp scissors will help you cut through the yarn easily, but make sure you use caution so you don't cut your fingers.

5| Trim the ends. Trim the ends of the pom-pom even for a uniform look. The shorter you cut the strands, the stiffer the pom-pom will be. For a more floppy pom-pom, leave the ends a bit longer. Use the tails from the square knot to tie the pom-pom onto your project.

Super Chunky Bracelets

This simple bracelet comes together in minutes, so don't stop at just one! Make a full set in coordinating colors that you can stack high on your wrist. Keep them casual by forming a closure with the yarn (see page 14), or go high end by using jewelry findings. Either way, the result will be fabulous!

DIFFICULTY:

APPROXIMATE LENGTH:
6" (15cm)

MATERIALS:
- 1 skein super bulky weight yarn

Yarn
The projects shown use Lion Brand® Yarn Hometown USA® (5oz./81yd. [142g/74m]), 1 skein each #100 New York White, #171 Key Lime, #400 Neon Pink.

Bracelet

1. Finger knit on 4 stitches until the work measures 5½" (15cm) or desired length. Bind off.

2. Form the final stitch of the bind-off tail into a closure as described on page 14.

Beaded Mod Necklace

This funky necklace is the perfect piece to pair with your favorite weekend outfit. Change up the beads and findings to create a completely different look!

DIFFICULTY:

APPROXIMATE LENGTH:
14" (35cm), excluding ties

MATERIALS:
- 1 skein worsted weight yarn
- 3 extra large metal mesh beads (about 25mm)
- 2 silver bead caps
- 1 silver hook-and-eye clasp

Necklace

1. Finger knit on 4 stitches for 12" (30cm), leaving long tails at the beginning and end for ties.

Assembly

1. Thread the 3 extra large mesh beads onto the finger knitting piece.

2. Thread each tail through 1 bead cap.

3. Tie on each side of the hook-and-eye clasp to the ties using double overhand knots, adjusting the placement of the claps as desired to adjust the length of the necklace.

4. Cut the remaining tails to 2" (5cm) and tie an overhand knot near the end of each one to prevent fraying.

Yarn
The project shown uses Lion Brand® Yarn Vanna's Choice®
(3.5oz./170yd. [100g/156m]), 1 skein #197 Sapphire.

Night Out Necklace

Finger knitting is so quick, it's easy to whip up jewelry pieces to match every outfit. With its shiny beads, this piece is perfect for a night out at a festive dinner or a party. For a more laid back look, check out the Beaded Mod Necklace on page 22.

DIFFICULTY: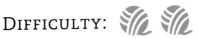

APPROXIMATE LENGTH:
16" (40cm), excluding ties

MATERIALS:
- 1 skein super bulky weight yarn
- 1 package metallic pony beads (9mm)
- Tapestry needle

Necklace

1. Using the tapestry needle, string 40 beads in random color order onto the yarn.

2. Cast on, leaving a long tail before the slip knot to use as a tie.

3. Finger knit on 4 stitches for 20 rows. On alternate rows, align 4 beads from the strand around the outside of your index finger. Make sure to pull the bottom loop over all 4 beads as you work the row.

4. Bind off, leaving a long tail as a tie.

Ties

1. Using the tapestry needle, string 10 beads onto each tail and tie a double overhand knot after them to hold them in place.

2. Trim the ties even.

3. Tie an overhand knot at the end of each tie to keep the yarn from fraying.

Yarn
The project shown uses Lion Brand® Yarn Wool-Ease® Thick & Quick® (6oz./106yd. [170g/97m]), 1 skein #153 Black.

Pom-Pom Scarf

Jazz up a piece of finger knitting with a fun pom-pom! Once you make one of these, you won't want to stop. Have fun mixing and matching colors of yarn. Keep the length short for an adorable necklace, or add length to make a scarf you can wrap around and around.

DIFFICULTY:

APPROXIMATE CIRCUMFERENCE:
30" (75cm)

MATERIALS:
- 2 skeins bulky weight yarn, 2 colors, 1 skein each color

Necklace

1. Using Color A, finger knit on 4 stitches until the work measures 30" (75cm) or desired length. Bind off.

Pom-Pom

1. Using Color B, make a 3" (7cm)-diameter pom-pom as shown on page 19.

Assembly

1. Sew the finger knitting into a loop.

2. Sew the pom-pom onto the finger knitting to cover the seam.

3. Weave in ends.

Switch colors as you knit (see page 12) to create different looks, like color blocking and stripes.

A pom-pom is not your only option! Attach any embellishment you want to your scarf.

Yarn
The project shown uses Lion Brand® Yarn Hometown USA®
(5oz./81yd. [142g/74m]), 1 skein #133 Syracuse Orange (Color
A), and Lion Brand® Yarn Hometown USA® (4 oz./64yd.
[113g/59m]), 1 skein #202 Circus (Color B).

Braided Scarf

Give your finger knitting a chunky look by braiding several strands together. The more strands you use, the thicker your scarf will be. Use the same color for each strand for a classic look, or use a different color for each strand for a playful twist.

DIFFICULTY:

APPROXIMATE LENGTH:
56" (140cm)

MATERIALS:
- 3 skeins bulky weight yarn, 3 colors, 1 skein each color

Finger Knitting

1. Using Color A, finger knit on 4 stitches until the work measures 80" (205cm) long or approximately 24" (60cm) longer than the desired finished scarf length. Repeat to make 2 additional pieces, 1 each in Colors B and C.

2. Weave in ends.

Scarf

1. Tie the 3 strands of finger knitting together near one end in an overhand knot.

2. Braid the 3 strands together until approximately 8" (20cm) remain unbraided.

3. Tie a second overhand knot near the unfinished end of the work.

Yarn
The project shown uses Lion Brand® Yarn Homespun® (6oz./185yd. [170g/169m]), 1 skein each #309 Deco (Color A), #404 Lagoon (Color B), #415 Pesto (Color C).

Button Love Scarf

If you're all about the embellishments, then this scarf is for you. The extra length allows you to style it tons of different ways, and you can always substitute beads or small pom-poms for the buttons if you'd like. Or try making flowers to add following the method described on page 17.

DIFFICULTY:

APPROXIMATE CIRCUMFERENCE:
6 yd. (600cm)

MATERIALS:
- 1 skein worsted weight yarn, 1 color (Color A)
- 2 skeins sport weight yarn, 1 color with sparkle (Color B)
- A variety of ¾"–1½" (19–38mm) buttons in coordinating colors and styles
- Tapestry needle

Scarf

1. Using 3 strands held together (1 strand Color A and 2 strands Color B), finger knit on 4 stitches until the work measures 6 yd. (600cm). Bind off.

2. Sew the finger knitting into a loop. Weave in ends.

3. Use yarn in Color B to sew buttons onto the finished scarf in a random pattern.

Yarn
The project shown uses Lion Brand® Yarn Vanna's Choice® (3.5oz./170yd. [100g/156m]), 1 skein #144 Magenta (Color A); Lion Brand® Yarn Vanna's Glamour® (1.75oz./202yd. [50g/185m]), 1 skein #146 Jewel (Color B); and Blumenthal Lansing, Favorite Findings Big Bag of Buttons, 1 bag each #2064 and #2003.

Statement Party Necklace

Love the look of a big chunky necklace, but don't want all the weight? Using finger knitting for your jewelry making is the perfect solution. This simple necklace captures the look of a statement piece without the extra weight, and the fuzzy yarn will feel great against your skin!

DIFFICULTY:

APPROXIMATE LENGTH:
36" (90cm) at longest point

MATERIALS:
- 3 skeins super bulky weight yarn, 3 colors, 1 skein each color
- 1 package sticky-backed hook-and-loop tape

Necklace

1. Using Color A, finger knit on 4 stitches for 20" (50cm). Bind off.

2. Using Color B, finger knit on 4 stitches for 28" (70cm). Bind off.

3. Using Color C, finger knit on 4 stitches for 36" (90cm). Bind off.

4. Weave in all ends.

Assembly

1. Arrange the finger knit pieces with the ends even in the order of A, B, C from left to right. Cut a piece of hook-and-loop tape the same length as the width of these 3 pieces and affix the hook side on top of the ends.

2. Turn the pieces 180 degrees so they are in the order of C, B, A from left to right. Even up the other set of ends, keeping the pieces parallel. Attach the loop side of the hook-and-loop tape to the underside of the ends.

Yarn

The project shown uses Lion Brand® Yarn Wool-Ease® Thick & Quick® (6oz./106yd. [170g/97m]), 1 skein each #303 Constellation (Color A), #301 Celebration (Color B), #306 Poinsettia (Color C).

Link Scarf

This is a showstopper that's sure to win you tons of compliments. And it's a great way to use up all the small amounts of yarn you might have left over in your stash from other projects. Have fun experimenting with different yarns and textures to create different looks. Bulky yarn will create stiff, chunky loops like chain, while thinner yarn will create more flexible loops that will lie like a necklace.

DIFFICULTY:

APPROXIMATE CIRCUMFERENCE:
30" (75cm)

MATERIALS:
- 1 skein super bulky weight yarn
- Tapestry needle

Links

1. Finger knit on 4 stitches for 18 rows. Bind off.

2. Repeat 8 times for a total of 9 links.

Assembly

1. Sew 1 link into a loop.

2. Thread a second link through the first and sew it into a loop. Repeat to add 6 more links, threading each one through the previous loop like links in a chain.

3. Thread the final link through the first and last loops of the chain and sew it into a loop to form the entire chain into a circle.

Yarn
The project shown uses Lion Brand® Yarn Wool-Ease® Thick & Quick® (6oz./106yd. [170g/97m]), 1 skein #153 Black.

Beaded Boho Belt

Bring some boho-chic style to your wardrobe with this earth-toned belt. The beaded fringe at the ends is a quick and easy way to add some extra flair. Pair it with a summertime dress or your favorite jeans and t-shirt!

DIFFICULTY:

APPROXIMATE LENGTH:
50" (125cm), excluding fringe

MATERIALS:
- 1 skein super bulky weight yarn
- 36 tan beads (14mm)
- 24 natural beads (10mm)
- 6 natural barrel beads (11 x 17mm)

Belt

1. Cast on 4 stitches, leaving a long tail for beading.

2. Finger knit until the work measures 50" (125cm) long or desired length. Bind off, leaving a long tail for beading.

Fringe

1. Cut 2 strands of yarn, each 28" (70cm) long.

2. Attach 1 strand to each end of the belt as shown on page 16.

3. Bead each strand as shown on page 16 using the following pattern for the beads: 1 red, 1 tan, 1 red, 1 tan, 1 red, 1 barrel, 1 red, 1 tan, 1 red, 1 tan, 1 red.

Yarn
The project shown uses Lion Brand® Yarn Wool-Ease® Thick & Quick® (6oz./106yd. [170g/97m]), 1 skein #501 Sequoia.

Chained Hairband with Flower

Combine finger knitting with finger chaining to create a simply sweet headband. Dress it up with an adorable flower embellishment or keep it plain and casual. Either way, you'll love how the soft yarn complements your hair.

DIFFICULTY:

APPROXIMATE LENGTH:
36" (90cm), including ties

MATERIALS:
- 1 skein worsted weight yarn
- 1⅛" (28mm) white textured shank button
- Tapestry needle

Headband

1. Finger knit on 4 stitches until the work measures 90" (230cm) long or desired length. Weave in ends.

2. Finger chain (see page 15), leaving 8" (20cm) tails at each end as ties.

Flower

1. Finger knit on 4 stitches until the work measures 28" (70cm) long.

2. Stitch the finger knitting into a flower as shown on page 17.

Assembly

1. Sew the flower onto the headband where desired.

Yarn
The project shown uses Lion Brand® Yarn Amazing® (1.75oz./147yd. [50g/135m]), 1 skein #200 Aurora, and La Petite 1⅛" (28mm) button, style #112.

Decorative Wreath

Wreaths are a great, customizable way to dress up a space, whether it's your office, your bedroom, your kitchen, or elsewhere. Make one for every season, or make just one and change the look by switching out the embellishments. There are so many different styles you can create!

DIFFICULTY:

APPROXIMATE DIAMETER:
13" (35cm)

MATERIALS:
- 2 skeins super bulky weight yarn, 1 color
- 12" (30cm) smooth foam wreath form
- Decorative clip-on embellishment of your choice
- Tapestry needle

Finger Knitting

1. Finger knit on 4 stitches until the work measures 10 yd. (10m). Bind off.

Assembly

1. Wrap the finger knitting around the circumference of the wreath by holding one end against the wreath and then bringing the other end through the center opening of the wreath from back to front. Repeat over and over until the two ends meet.

2. Sew the two ends together.

3. Attach the embellishment.

Yarn
The project shown uses Lion Brand® Yarn Wool-Ease® Thick & Quick® (6oz./106yd. [170g/97m]), 2 skeins #131 Grass.

Delightful Home Dec Set

Finger knitting is not just for wearables! Sew the edges of a piece of finger knitting together in a circle to create cute coasters that are perfect for any dorm or apartment. Or use the same technique on a larger scale to make an extra soft rug that will feel great under your toes. Long pieces of finger knitting can be used to add monograms or words to throw pillows for a unique, personalized touch. Choose a color palette to match your personal taste and style, like bright neons for a fun and funky dorm room or classic neutrals for a sophisticated first-time apartment.

Cozy Coasters

DIFFICULTY:

APPROXIMATE DIAMETER:
4½" (11cm)

MATERIALS:
- 3 skeins super bulky weight yarn, 3 colors, 1 skein each color
- Tapestry needle

Coasters

1. Using Color A, finger knit on 4 stitches until the work measures 18" (45cm). Bind off, leaving a long tail for sewing. Repeat to make 5 additional pieces, 1 more in Color A and 2 each in Colors B and C for 6 total.

Finishing

1. Sew each strip into a coil as described on page 14. Weave in ends.

Yarn
The project shown uses Lion Brand® Yarn Hometown USA® (5oz./81yd. [142g/74m]), 1 skein each #400 Neon Pink (Color A), #401 Neon Orange (Color B), #402 Neon Yellow (Color C).

Spiral Rug

Rug

1. Using Color A, finger knit on 4 stitches for 12 rows.

2. Switch to Color B (see page 12) and finger knit for 12 rows.

3. Switch to Color C and finger knit for 12 rows.

4. Continue to finger knit in this color order (12 rows A, 12 rows B, 12 rows C) until the work measures approximately 10 yd. (10m) long or desired length.

Assembly

1. Sew the finger knitting into a coil following the instructions on page 14, changing the color of the sewing yarn as needed to hide the stitches.

DIFFICULTY:

APPROXIMATE DIAMETER:
17" (45cm)

MATERIALS:
- 3 skeins super bulky weight yarn, 3 colors, 1 skein each color
- Tapestry needle

Yarn

The project shown uses Lion Brand® Yarn Hometown USA® (5oz./81yd. [142g/74m]), 1 skein each #400 Neon Pink (Color A), #401 Neon Orange (Color B), #402 Neon Yellow (Color C).

Positive Vibes Throw Pillow

Create a custom throw pillow with a favorite word spelled out in finger knitting. What you choose to spell is completely up to you! Use your name or initials, or pick a special word that will make you smile. Or create a set of pillows with complementary words like LIVE, LAUGH, LOVE.

Lettering

1. Finger knit on 3 stitches only for 60" (150cm). Bind off. Weave in ends.

Front

1. Cut a piece of fleece 17" (43cm) square. Place a straight pin at the center.

2. Arrange the finger knitting piece to spell out JOY, making sure the centered straight pin is in the center of the O.

3. Using the sewing needle and thread, stitch the finger knitting in place.

Back

1. Cut 2 pieces of white fleece, each 17" x 11" (43 x 28cm).

2. Turn back 2" (5cm) along one 17" (43cm) side of each piece and fold the cut edge under. With the sewing machine and white thread, stitch the hems in place. You will have 2 pieces, each 17" x 9" (43 x 23cm).

3. Overlap the hemmed edges of the 2 pieces by 1" (3cm) to form a 17" (43cm) square. Pin the overlapped hemmed edges together.

Assembly

1. Place the front and back pieces together with wrong sides facing and pin around the edges. Sew around the entire perimeter using a ½" (1.5cm) seam allowance.

2. Clip the corners and turn the pillow cover right side out through the hemmed overlap.

Finishing

1. Make 4 tassels following the instructions on page 18. Stitch one tassel to each corner of the pillow.

2. Insert the pillow form through the hemmed slit in the back of the pillow. Affix 3 self-adhesive hook-and-loop tape dots to the hemmed edges to keep the pillow opening closed. You can also cut 1" (2.5cm) hook-and-loop tape strips for this.

Yarn
The project shown uses Lion Brand® Yarn Hometown USA®
(5oz./81yd. [142g/74m]), 1 skein #400 Neon Pink.

Project Index

Gallery Projects

Beaded Mod Necklace
Pages 7 and 22–23
Lion Brand® Yarn Vanna's Choice®
(3.5oz./170yd. [100g/156m]), 1 skein
#197 Sapphire

Beaded Boho Belt
Pages 36–37
Lion Brand® Yarn Wool-Ease® Thick &
Quick® (6oz./106yd. [170g/97m]), 1 skein
#501 Sequoia

Braided Scarf
Front cover and pages 28–29
Lion Brand® Yarn Homespun®
(6oz./185yd. [170g/169m]), 1 skein each
#309 Deco (Color A), #404 Lagoon (Color
B), #415 Pesto (Color C)

Button Love Scarf
Back cover and pages 30–31
Lion Brand® Yarn Vanna's Choice®
(3.5oz./170yd. [100g/156m]), 1 skein #144
Magenta (Color A)
Lion Brand® Yarn Vanna's Glamour®
(1.75oz./202yd. [50g/185m]), 1 skein #146
Jewel (Color B)
Blumenthal Lansing, Favorite Findings Big
Bag of Buttons, 1 bag each #2064 and
#2003

Chained Hairband with Flower
Back cover and pages 17 and 38–39
Lion Brand® Yarn Amazing®
(1.75oz./147yd. [50g/135m]), 1 skein
#200 Aurora
La Petite 1⅛" (28mm) button, style #112

Cozy Coasters
Pages 43–44
Lion Brand® Yarn Hometown USA®
(5oz./81yd. [142g/74m]), 1 skein each #400
Neon Pink, #401 Neon Orange, #402
Neon Yellow

Decorative Wreath
Pages 40–41
Lion Brand® Yarn Wool-Ease® Thick &
Quick® (6oz./106yd. [170g/97m]), 2 skeins
#131 Grass

Link Scarf
Pages 34–35
Lion Brand® Yarn Wool-Ease® Thick &
Quick® (6oz./106yd. [170g/97m]), 1 skein
#153 Black

Night Out Necklace
Back cover and pages 2–3 and 24–25
Lion Brand® Yarn Wool-Ease® Thick &
Quick® (6oz./106yd. [170g/97m]), 1 skein
#153 Black
Assorted metallic pony beads

Pom-Pom Scarf
Back cover and pages 6 and 26–27
Lion Brand® Yarn Hometown USA®
(5oz./81yd. [142g/74m]), 1 skein #133
Syracuse Orange (Color A)
Lion Brand® Yarn Hometown USA® (4
oz./64yd. [113g/59m]), 1 skein #202 Circus
(Color B)

Positive Vibes Throw Pillow
Front cover and pages 42 and 46–47
Lion Brand® Yarn Hometown USA®
(5oz./81yd. [142g/74m]), 1 skein #400
Neon Pink

Spiral Rug
Pages 43 and 45
Lion Brand® Yarn Hometown USA®
(5oz./81yd. [142g/74m]), 1 skein each #400
Neon Pink (Color A), #401 Neon Orange
(Color B), #402 Neon Yellow (Color C)

Statement Party Necklace
Front cover and pages 32–33
Lion Brand® Yarn Wool-Ease® Thick &
Quick® (6oz./106yd. [170g/97m]), 1 skein
each #303 Constellation (Color A), #301
Celebration (Color B), #306 Poinsettia
(Color C)

Super Chunky Bracelets
Pages 8 and 20–21
Lion Brand® Yarn Hometown USA®
(5oz./81yd. [142g/74m]), 1 skein each #100
New York White, #171 Key Lime, #400
Neon Pink

Interior front cover and page 4
Lion Brand® Yarn Wool-Ease® (3
oz./197 yd. [85g/180m], 1 skein
#153 Black
Silver Creek Leather Company Safari
leather bracelet blank
4 jump rings

Pages 5 and 12
Lion Brand® Yarn Wool-Ease® (3
oz./197 yd. [85g/180m], 1 skein #194
Denim Twist

Page 8 (necklace)
Lion Brand® Yarn Hometown USA®
(5oz./81yd. [142g/74m]), 1 skein #400
Neon Pink.
1½" (4cm)-wide zebra print ribbon
⅝" (1.5cm)-wide zebra print ribbon
Sewing needle and white thread

Pages 11 and 26 (right)
Lion Brand® Yarn Hometown USA®
(5oz./81yd. [142g/74m]), 1 skein each
#194 Monterey Lime, #107 Charlotte
Blue, #100 New York White

Page 26 (left)
Lion Brand® Yarn Hometown USA®
(5oz./81yd. [142g/74m]), 1 skein #194
Monterey Lime
Light purple, purple, and yellow felt
Yellow embroidery floss

Interior back cover
Lion Brand® Yarn Wool-Ease® (3
oz./197 yd. [85g/180m]), 1 skein
#153 Black
4mm and 6mm Swarovski round pearls
in Powder Almond
3mm Czech glass round crystals
Black thread
Silver chain and clasp

Tip
Check out *www.arm-knitting.com*
for videos, tips, and tricks on
finger knitting!